The Possum Magic Cookbook

Illustrated by Julie Vivas

Based on *Possum Magic* by Mem Fox and Julie Vivas

Compiled by Gina Inverarity and Celia Jellett

An Omnibus Book from Scholastic Australia

Omnibus Books
175–177 Young Street, Parkside SA 5063
an imprint of Scholastic Australia Pty Ltd (ABN 11 000 614 577)
PO Box 579, Gosford NSW 2250.
www.scholastic.com.au

Part of the Scholastic Group
Sydney • Auckland • New York • Toronto • London • Mexico City •
New Delhi • Hong Kong • Buenos Aires • Puerto Rico

First published in 1985 as *The Grandma Poss Cookbook*.
Revised edition first published in 2015.
Reprinted in 2015 (twice).
Text copyright © Omnibus Books, 1985, 2015.
Illustrations copyright © Julie Vivas, 1983, 1985, 2012, 2014, 2015.

All rights reserved. No part of this publication may be reproduced or transmitted in any form
or by any means, electronic or mechanical, including photocopying, recording,
storage in an information retrieval system, or otherwise, without the prior written permission
of the publisher, unless specifically permitted under the Australian Copyright Act 1968 as amended.

National Library of Australia Cataloguing-in-Publication entry

Title: The Possum Magic cookbook / illustrated by Julie Vivas;
based on *Possum Magic* by Mem Fox and Julie Vivas

ISBN 978 1 74299 121 4 (hardback)
Target Audience: For primary school age.
Subjects: Cooking – Juvenile literature.
Cooking, Australian – Juvenile literature.
Animals – Juvenile literature.

Dewey Number: 641.5994

Typeset in Berkeley.
Julie Vivas used watercolours to create the illustrations for this book.
Printed and bound by Tien Wah Press (Pte.) Ltd.

10 9 8 7 6 5 4 3   15 16 17 18 19 20/ 0

Contents

Savouries

Double Decker Sandwiches	1
Easy Peasy Pizza	2
Funny Dip Echidna	4
Minty Pea Toasties	5
Cheese Straws	6
Twirly Whirlys	8
Tasty Sausage Rolls	10

Sweets

Pumpkin Scones	12
Anzac Biscuits	14
Fruit Rockets	15
Honey Crackles	16
Chocolate Birthday Cake	18
Lamingtons	20
Pavlova	22
Frog Jelly	25
Sparkle Biscuits	26
Apple Fizz Drink	28

Double Decker Sandwiches
Easy for kids

6 slices white bread
6 slices wholemeal bread
butter for spreading
3 eggs, boiled
1 tablespoon butter, softened
Vegemite
lettuce leaves
3 slices ham

Butter all the slices of bread and cut off the crusts. Peel the boiled eggs and mash them in a bowl with the tablespoon of softened butter. Spread some egg mixture on a slice of white bread and top with a slice of wholemeal bread. Lightly butter the top side and spread with Vegemite. Lay some lettuce on top of the Vegemite, then another slice of white bread followed by ham and a slice of buttered wholemeal bread.
Repeat for the other two stacks. Wrap tightly in foil and refrigerate until needed. To serve, unwrap the sandwiches and cut each stack carefully into four longways slices.

Makes 12 sandwiches

Easy Peasy Pizza
Easy for kids

6 small pita breads
⅓ cup tomato paste
150 g ham, roast chicken or salami
(for vegetarians substitute a cup of pumpkin, chopped into small cubes and roasted in the oven in olive oil and salt until soft)
2 ripe tomatoes, chopped
1 capsicum, red or green
button mushrooms, sliced
1 cup cheese, grated

Preheat oven to 180°C. Line two oven trays with baking paper. Spread the pita breads with tomato paste and then place them on the trays. Sprinkle the meat (or pumpkin) over each pita bread. Add the other toppings and finish with the cheese. Bake for 8 to 10 minutes or until crisp and the cheese melts. Remove them from the oven, and when they are a little cooler cut each pizza into four slices and serve.

Makes 24 slices

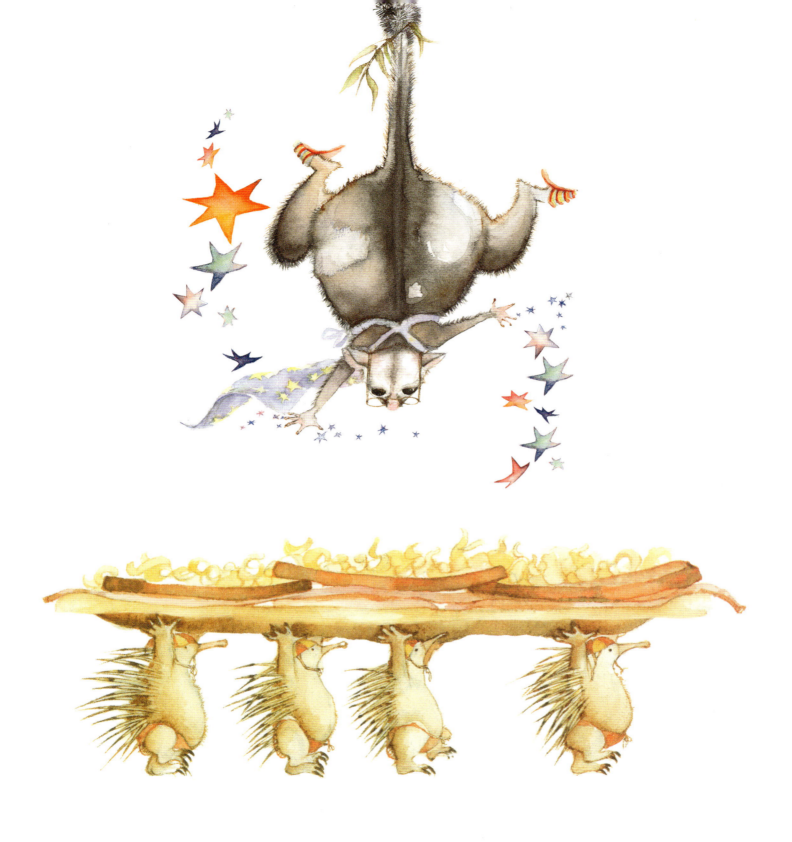

Funny Dip Echidna
Easy for kids

1 large avocado
1 clove garlic, crushed
¼ cup either sour cream or plain yogurt
2 tablespoons lemon juice
salt and pepper
olives, celery or cheese for decorating
carrot, celery or cucumber, cut into matchstick shapes

Mash together the avocado, crushed garlic, sour cream or yogurt, lemon juice and some salt and pepper to taste. Try to make it nice and smooth, but a few lumps won't matter. When it's all mashed, make a mound on a plate in a large egg shape. At the front of the mound make eyes and a nose using olives and shapes you cut from cucumber or cheese. Then poke the thin vegetable sticks into the mound of dip as if they are spines on an echidna.

Serves 6 to 8

Minty Pea Toasties
Some help from a grown-up

1 cup frozen peas, thawed
½ avocado
4–5 mint leaves, chopped
1 small clove garlic, crushed
1 tablespoon extra virgin olive oil
squeeze of lemon juice
salt and pepper
1 baguette, cut into thin slices
extra peas and mint leaves for garnishing

Mash together or combine peas, avocado, mint, garlic, olive oil, lemon juice and salt and pepper in a food processor. Toast baguette slices lightly and spread with minty pea mixture. Garnish with a few peas and mint leaves.

Makes approximately 24 toasties

Cheese Straws
Some help from a grown-up

1 cup self-raising flour
salt and pepper
60 g butter
¾ cup cheese
50 ml cold water
extra flour

Set oven temperature at 200°C and line two oven trays with baking paper. Sift flour, salt and pepper into a bowl and add butter, gently combining with your fingers until the mixture resembles breadcrumbs. (You can also do this in a food processor.) Add the cheese to the flour mixture and combine, then add the water a little at a time to make the dough hold together without being sticky. Sprinkle some flour on your hands and the table top. Work the dough until it is a smooth ball. Roll out the pastry to an even 5 millimetres thick then cut into strips about 1 centimetre wide and 8 centimetres long and lay them carefully on the oven trays. Bake for about 10 minutes, until they are golden brown. Place on a wire rack to cool.

Serves 6 to 10

Twirly Whirlys
Some help from a grown-up

You can make any kind of Twirly Whirly just by choosing the things you like best to go inside. They can have meat or vegetables or both.

1 teaspoon Dijon mustard
1 tablespoon mayonnaise
half a roasted chicken, or any cooked meat
½ avocado, peeled
1 medium tomato
2 flour tortillas
½ cup carrot, grated
½ cup alfalfa sprouts or chopped lettuce

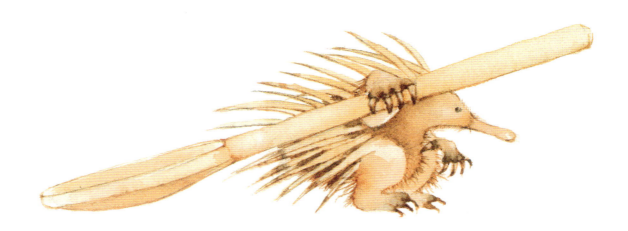

In a small dish, stir together the mustard and mayonnaise. Chop the chicken into small chunks. Cut the avocado and tomato into small pieces. Microwave each tortilla for 30 seconds, uncovered, on high. Spread the tortilla with the mayonnaise mix and then put your filling in the middle. Leave a space around the edges. Fold the sides towards the middle and, holding the tortilla at the bottom edge, roll it up tightly. Wrap this in foil and cut it into slices about 4 centimetres wide when you are ready to serve.

Makes 8

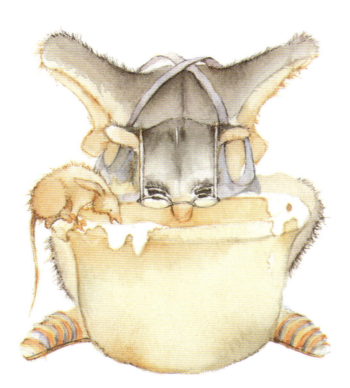

Tasty Sausage Rolls
Some help from a grown-up

3 sheets puff pastry
12 good-quality beef sausages
1 egg, beaten
sesame seeds

Set oven temperature at 200°C. Line an oven tray with baking paper. Cut a sheet of pastry in quarters and brush the edges with beaten egg. (How big you cut the pastry will depend on how big your sausages are.) Roll one sausage in each pastry square, pinching and crimping the edges shut. Cut in half and then brush all over with egg and sprinkle with sesame seeds. Place sausage rolls on the oven tray and bake in a hot oven for 20 to 25 minutes. If the pastry browns too quickly, cover the sausage rolls with some foil. Serve warm with tomato sauce.

Makes 24

Pumpkin Scones
Some help from a grown-up

60 g butter
¼ cup caster sugar
1 cup pumpkin, cooked and mashed
1 egg
2½ cups self-raising flour
½ teaspoon salt
½ cup milk
extra flour and milk

Set oven temperature at 220°C and line an oven tray with baking paper. Combine butter and sugar and then add the mashed pumpkin and the egg. Sift the flour and salt together over the bowl and gently mix it in. Add the milk to form a soft, but not sticky, dough. (More flour or more milk may be needed.)

Sprinkle a little flour on the bench, turn dough out
and work it a little until it is smooth. Pat out to
a 2-centimetre thickness. Cut scones using
a floured glass upside down. Gather the scraps together
and pat the dough out again. Repeat until all the dough
is used up. Place the scones on the oven tray about
1 centimetre apart and brush tops with milk.
Cook for about 15 minutes or until the tops
are golden brown.

Makes 12 scones

Anzac Biscuits

Some help from a grown-up

1 cup rolled oats
1 cup plain flour
1 cup sugar
¾ cup desiccated coconut
125 g butter
1 tablespoon golden syrup
2 tablespoons boiling water
1½ teaspoons bicarbonate of soda

Set oven temperature at 160°C and line two oven trays with baking paper. Combine rolled oats, flour, sugar and coconut in a mixing bowl. Melt butter and golden syrup in a small saucepan. When it is bubbling set aside. Measure boiling water into a cup, add in the bicarbonate of soda and then quickly combine it with the butter and golden syrup mixture. While it is still frothing, pour the mixture over the dry ingredients. Stir well. Drop teaspoonfuls of the mixture onto the oven trays about 4 centimetres apart. Bake for 20 minutes or until golden brown. Remove the trays from the oven and leave biscuits on the trays to cool and become crisp.

Makes 36 biscuits

Fruit Rockets
Easy for kids

Choose any six fruits
you really like, but they must be
able to be cut into chunks
or easily pierced and still stay in one piece.

rockmelon
watermelon
grapes
strawberries
mango
pineapple
apple
pear
marshmallows
bamboo skewers

Cut the fruit into bite-sized pieces. Thread the fruit pieces
onto skewers, to make a 'rocket', with one marshmallow
at the top and bottom of each stick.

Honey Crackles
Some help from a grown-up

4 cups cornflakes
100 g butter
3 tablespoons honey

Arrange 24 patty pans on an oven tray.
Set the oven temperature to 140°C.
Measure the cornflakes into a mixing bowl.
Place the butter and honey in a saucepan
over low heat until completely melted.
Let it bubble for a few seconds and then
take it off the stove. Pour the hot liquid
over the cornflakes and mix carefully without
crushing the cornflakes. All the flakes
should be well coated. Spoon cornflake mix
into the patty pans until they are full.
Place the tray in the oven and cook for
about 10 minutes. Set aside to cool
before serving.

Makes 24 crackles

17

Chocolate Birthday Cake
Some help from a grown-up

200 g butter
200 g caster sugar
3 eggs
200 g self-raising flour
1 teaspoon baking powder
50 g cocoa
2 tablespoons milk
1 teaspoon vanilla essence

Line two 20-centimetre cake tins with baking paper. Set oven temperature at 180°C. Cream butter and sugar together until light and fluffy using an electric beater if you have one. Add eggs one at a time, combining well. Sift in dry ingredients and lastly add milk and vanilla essence. Mix well. Divide the mixture between the two tins and bake for 35 minutes or until a skewer inserted in the middle comes out clean. Turn the cakes onto a wire rack to cool.

Icing and filling

50 g softened butter
1 tablespoon cocoa
1½ cups icing sugar
2 tablespoons hot water
strawberry or raspberry jam
hundreds and thousands or
chocolate sprinkles

Combine butter, cocoa and icing sugar.
Add water slowly, whisking together until
the icing is a nice spreadable consistency.
Put one of the cakes on the serving plate
upside down. Spread it with jam.
Rest the other cake on top of the jam,
right side up. Spread the icing over the top
and sides of the cake with a flat knife.
Finish with hundreds and thousands or
chocolate sprinkles.

Serves approximately 16

Lamingtons
Some help from a grown-up

Lamingtons are traditionally made over two days, cooking the cake on the first day and dipping the cake squares in chocolate icing the day after. If you try to make lamingtons with fresh cake they may fall apart. You will need a lamington tray about 30 x 25 centimetres with sides about 3 centimetres high. Or if you're in a hurry you can buy plain sponge cakes from the supermarket and skip to the instructions for icing.

For the cake

125 g butter, softened
1 cup caster sugar
½ teaspoon vanilla essence
3 eggs
1¾ cups self-raising flour, sifted
½ cup milk

Set the oven temperature to 165°C. Line the lamington pan with baking paper. Put the butter, sugar and vanilla in a bowl and beat with an electric beater until it is pale and fluffy. Add the eggs one at a time and beat just until they are incorporated. Add half the flour and half the milk and mix gently using a wooden spoon. Add the other half of the milk and flour, stirring until smooth. Pour mixture into the tray and bake for 30 minutes or until golden. Test by sticking a skewer into the middle. If it comes out clean the cake is done. When it is cool lift the cake out by the paper onto a cooling rack. Cover and leave until the next day.

For the chocolate icing

3½ cups icing sugar, sifted
¼ cup cocoa powder, sifted
1 tablespoon butter, softened
½ cup hot water
2 cups desiccated coconut

Cut the cake into even-sized cubes or fingers.
You should get about 15. Put the sifted icing sugar,
cocoa powder and butter in a bowl and add the hot water.
Mix until it is smooth. Use a skewer or a fork to dip
the squares of cake into the icing. Let the extra drip off,
then roll the squares in coconut. Dry them on the rack.

Makes approximately 15 lamingtons

Pavlova

Some help from a grown-up

Any kind of fruit is good for decorating a pavlova – strawberries, bananas, kiwifruit, peaches or pineapple.

2 eggs
¾ cup caster sugar
vanilla essence
oil

Set the oven temperature to 120°C. Line a flat tray with baking paper. Trace a 20-centimetre circle in the middle with pencil. Brush inside the circle with cooking oil. Wipe out a mixing bowl to make sure it is dry and clean. (The egg whites will not beat into a froth if there is any grease in the bowl.) Separate the eggs and add the whites to the bowl, being very careful not to let any yolk contaminate the whites. Whisk until the egg whites form stiff peaks. Add caster sugar and a few drops of vanilla essence gradually and whisk until the mixture is thick and glossy. Spoon the mixture onto the tray, making a smooth shape inside the circle. Slide the tray into the oven and cook for 1½ hours. Let the pavlova cool before decorating.

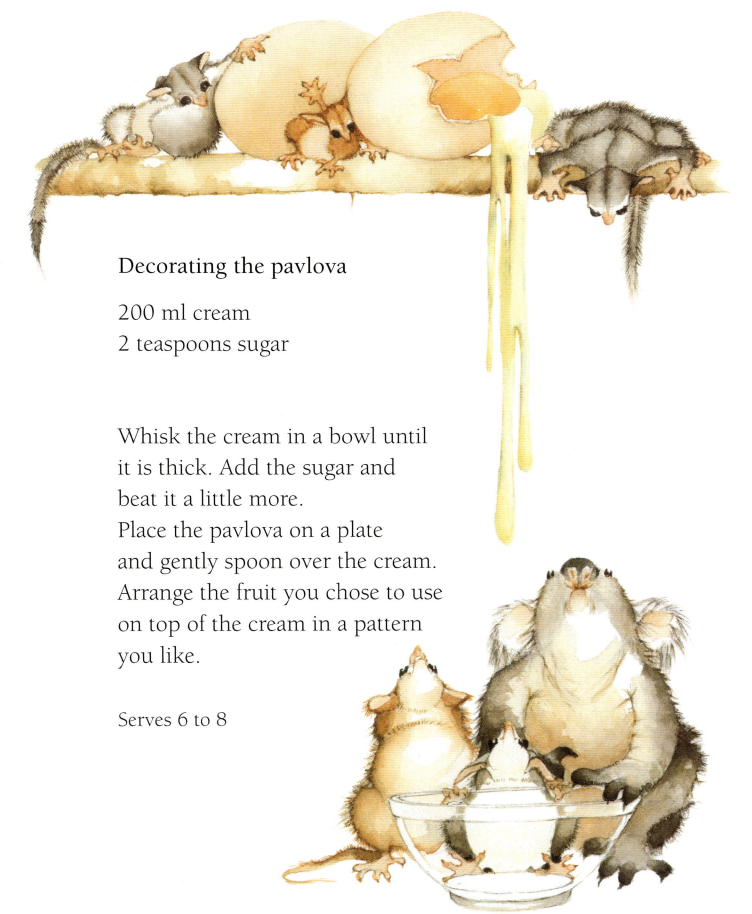

Decorating the pavlova

200 ml cream
2 teaspoons sugar

Whisk the cream in a bowl until it is thick. Add the sugar and beat it a little more.
Place the pavlova on a plate and gently spoon over the cream. Arrange the fruit you chose to use on top of the cream in a pattern you like.

Serves 6 to 8

Frog Jelly
Some help from a grown-up

2 packets green jelly crystals
nasturtium leaves (or any other edible leaves)
chocolate frogs

Prepare the jelly following the instructions on the packet. Pour into a large pond-shaped bowl and place in the fridge to set. When the jelly is set, trim the stalks off the nasturtium leaves and arrange them on top of the jelly with a chocolate frog on top of each one.

Sparkle Biscuits
Some help from a grown-up

125 g butter
1 cup caster sugar
1 egg
½ teaspoon vanilla essence
1 cup self-raising flour
1 cup plain flour

Line two oven trays with paper and set oven temperature to 180°C. In a food processor cream the butter and sugar and then add egg and vanilla essence. Sift in self-raising flour and plain flour and mix until a smooth dough forms. Tip onto a floured surface and roll out to 1-centimetre thickness. Cut shapes using cookie cutters. Carefully arrange the biscuits on the trays, leaving space between them. Bake for 15 to 20 minutes or until lightly golden. Set aside to cool.

Decorating the biscuits

1 cup icing sugar
hot water
hundreds and thousands

In a bowl, add hot water to the icing sugar
a few drops at a time until it forms a thick
smooth icing. Spread on cooled biscuits
and then sprinkle with hundreds and thousands.

Makes approximately 24

Apple Fizz Drink
Easy for kids

1 small apple
vanilla ice cream
apple juice
mineral or soda water

Peel the apple and cut some thin slices.
Place a scoop of ice cream in a glass and pour in some apple juice, leaving some space at the top. Fill the glass with the fizzy water and decorate with apple slices.

Serves 1

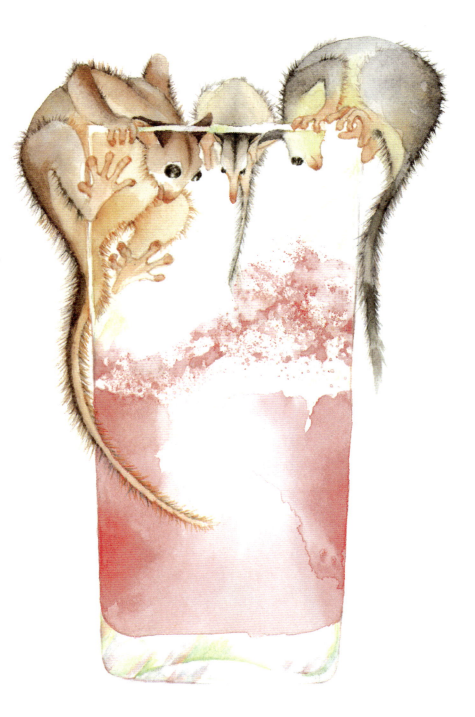

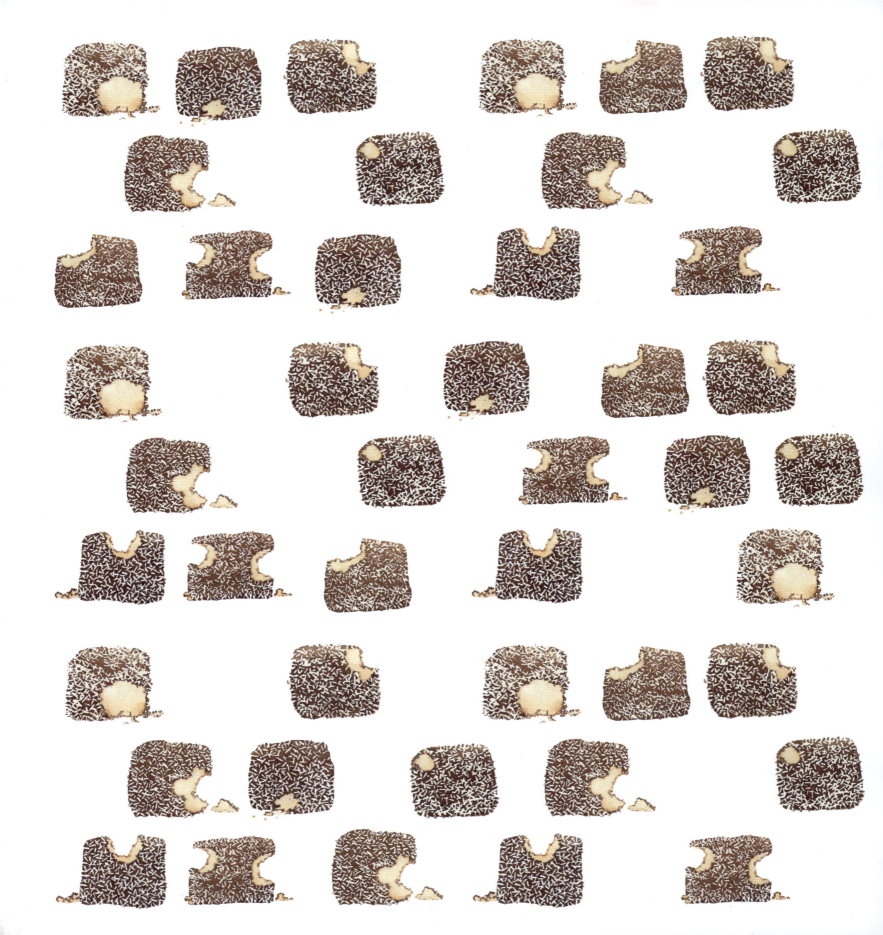